WORLD ABOUT US
RECYCLING

TONY HARE

GLOUCESTER PRESS
New York London Toronto Sydney

© Aladdin Books Ltd 1991

First published in
the United States in 1991 by
Gloucester Press
387 Park Avenue South
New York NY 10016

Design: David West
Children's
Book Design
Editor: Fiona Robertson
Illustrator: Simon Bishop
Consultant: Jo Gordon

Library of Congress Cataloging-
in-Publication Data

Hare, Tony.
Recycling / by Tony Hare.
p. cm.--(World about us)
Includes index.
Summary: Discusses methods of recycling metal, plastic, paper, and glass, and why such conservation efforts are important.
ISBN 0-531-17352-6
1. Recycling (Waste, etc.)--
Juvenile literature.
2. Conservation of natural resources--Juvenile literature.
3. Pollution--Juvenile literature.
[1. Recycling (waste)
2. Conservation of natural resources.] I. Title. II. Series.
TD794.5.H37   1991
363.72'82--dc20
91-11579   CIP   AC

Printed in Belgium
All rights reserved

Contents

Why recycle?
4
Natural recycling
6
Waste
8
Out of control
10
Looking back
12
Recycling today
14
Industry
16
Energy from waste
18
Plastics
20
Recycling worldwide
22
What can you do?
24
Making it work
26
Did you know?
28
Glossary
31
Index
32

Introduction

Recycling means putting waste back into use. This can be done by reusing all or some of the materials that are used to make products. Today, the number of products that end up as waste is rapidly increasing. Simply throwing things away when a person has finished with them not only pollutes the environment, but also wastes the earth's precious raw materials. Recycling is being seen as an important solution to these problems.

Why recycle?

Recycling and reusing things helps to save the earth's precious raw materials, or resources. Many of the resources used to make the things we buy, like oil for plastic and metal for cars, are nonrenewable. This means that the earth only has a limited supply of them. In addition, some nonrenewable resources, like coal, oil, and gas, are used to provide the energy needed for goods and services.

The energy needed to manufacture most products comes from fuels like coal (below). But when coal is burned it gives out gases that pollute the air.

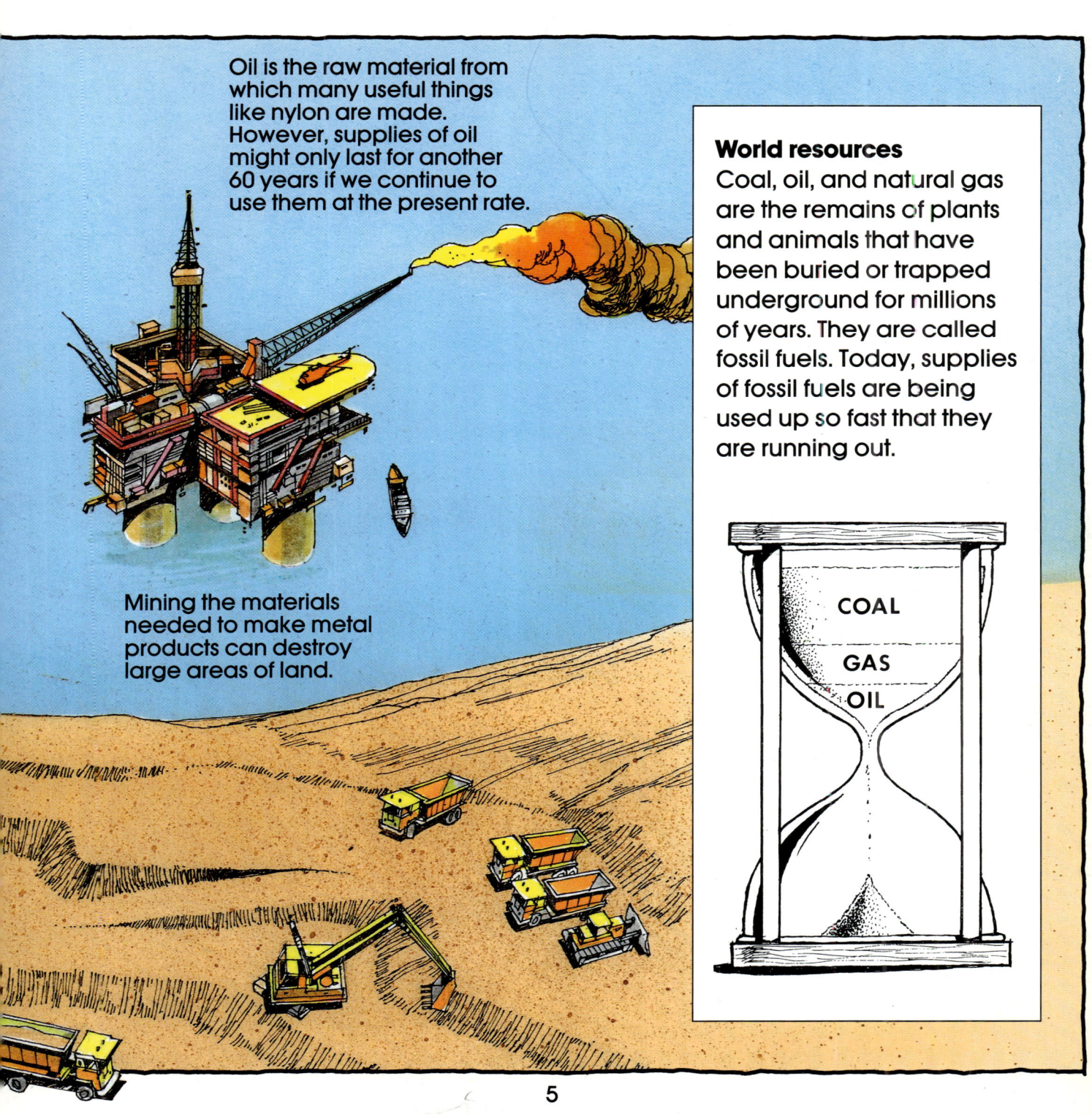

Oil is the raw material from which many useful things like nylon are made. However, supplies of oil might only last for another 60 years if we continue to use them at the present rate.

Mining the materials needed to make metal products can destroy large areas of land.

World resources

Coal, oil, and natural gas are the remains of plants and animals that have been buried or trapped underground for millions of years. They are called fossil fuels. Today, supplies of fossil fuels are being used up so fast that they are running out.

COAL
GAS
OIL

Natural recycling

In the natural world, all the waste produced by living things is recycled. Animal droppings and dead bodies are broken down by small creatures in the soil, like worms, to provide "food" for other living things. The carbon dioxide that people and animals breathe out is taken up by plants and used to make the substances they need to grow. Plants give out oxygen, which people and animals need to breathe.

Plants take up water through their roots and pass it out through their leaves as moisture. This moisture, along with water vapor from rivers and seas rises to form clouds.

Water that is not used by living things eventually returns to the river or sea, to be reused all over again.

Waste

Waste is anything we no longer want, from the food scraps we throw into the garbage can to the chemical poisons left over from industry. The problem of waste is made worse by the "throwaway" attitude of many people. Products bought today are often made to be used just once, and then thrown away. Many products are wrapped in unnecessary packaging which ends up as waste when the goods are unwrapped.

Garbage from our homes is usually buried in the ground in landfill sites. It can then pollute the water supplies underground if harmful materials from the site seep into the ground.

Many old cookers, refrigerators, and washing machines are dumped every year.

Out of control

Over the last 100 years, many new materials have been developed, like plastics, detergents, and chemical pesticides. Although such products are very useful, many of them cannot be broken down naturally. Once produced, they can stay in the environment for many years. Plastic bottles pile up on our garbage dumps, and chemical poisons can get into our food and water supply.

The rising number of cars means that vast amounts of precious resources, like steel, are being used up.

A large amount of domestic waste is packaging. Cans, paper, and plastics all end up as waste, on garbage dumps, or left lying on the street.

Many of the things in our society today are made to be convenient and produce a lot of waste, like the containers used in fast-food stores.

Of the millions of tons of paper used every year, only a fraction is recycled.

Looking back

Although only a fraction of our waste is recycled at the moment, recycling is not a new idea. The metal and building industries have long reused the slate tiles found on roofs and metals like lead. For years, jumble sales and thrift shops have sold old clothes and other items.

In some countries, a small amount of money, called a deposit, is paid when bottles are returned. The bottles are melted down and the glass is reused.

All different kinds of paper, from newspapers to magazines to writing paper, can be recycled, and people have been doing so for many years.

Metals like copper, which is used to make pipes, are valuable. Items that contain metal can be collected, melted down and used for new products.

Recycling glass
Empty glass bottles can be returned to glass factories where they are sorted out into different colors. The glass is then broken up to make cullet, which can then be used to make new glass.

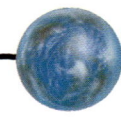

Recycling today

One of the major problems with recycling is separating the useful materials, like paper, glass, and metals, from the rest of our garbage. There are recycling plants where mixed garbage can be sorted. But it is much better if the garbage is not mixed in the first place, which means that we must sort it at home. In some places, the different materials are collected separately.

Magnets collect iron and steel items. Other metals, along with glass and some plastics, are also sorted out and collected to be taken away for recycling.

At modern waste processing plants air is blown over the waste so that light materials like paper drift off and can be collected.

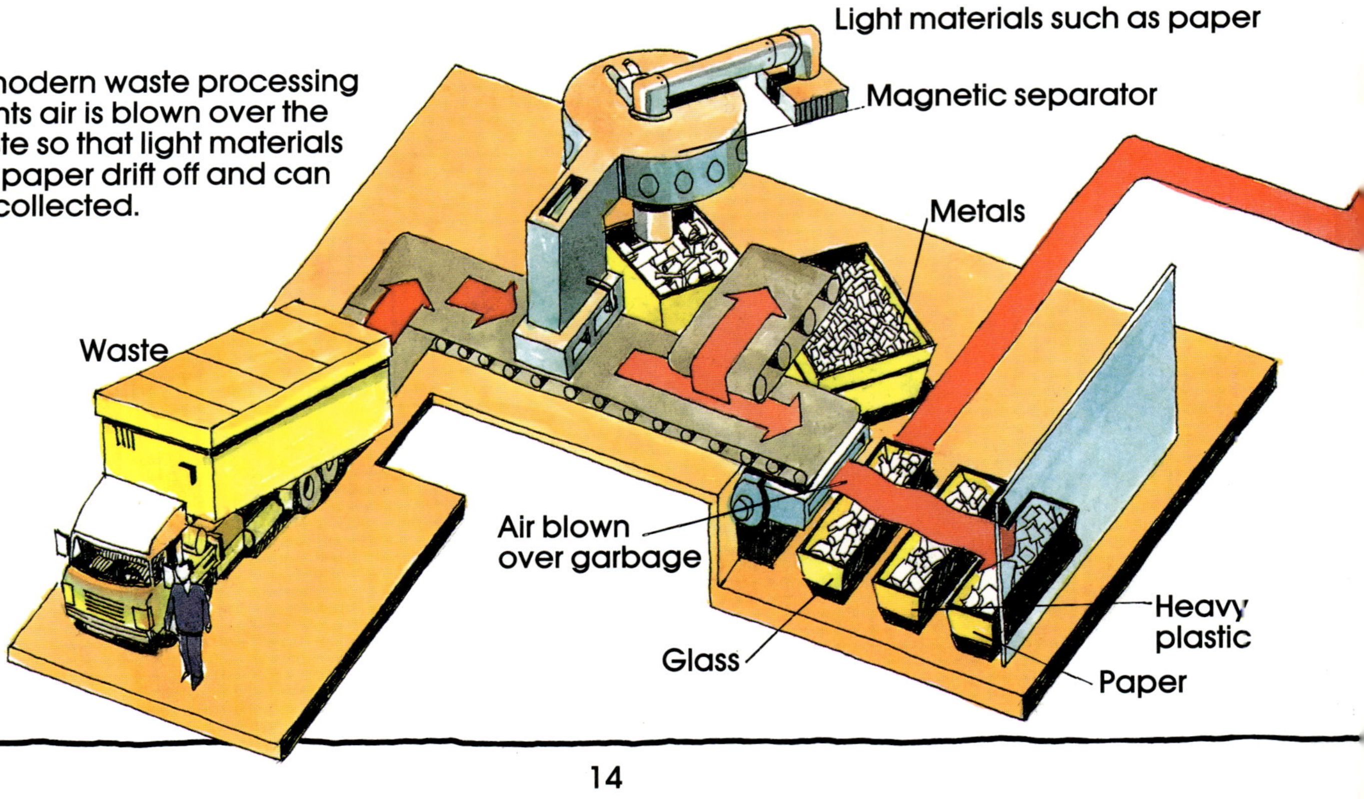

Waste

Light materials such as paper

Magnetic separator

Metals

Air blown over garbage

Glass

Heavy plastic

Paper

Recycling cans
Recycling the metal aluminum, which is used in some drinks cans, saves up to 95 percent of the energy that is needed to make a new product from the raw materials.

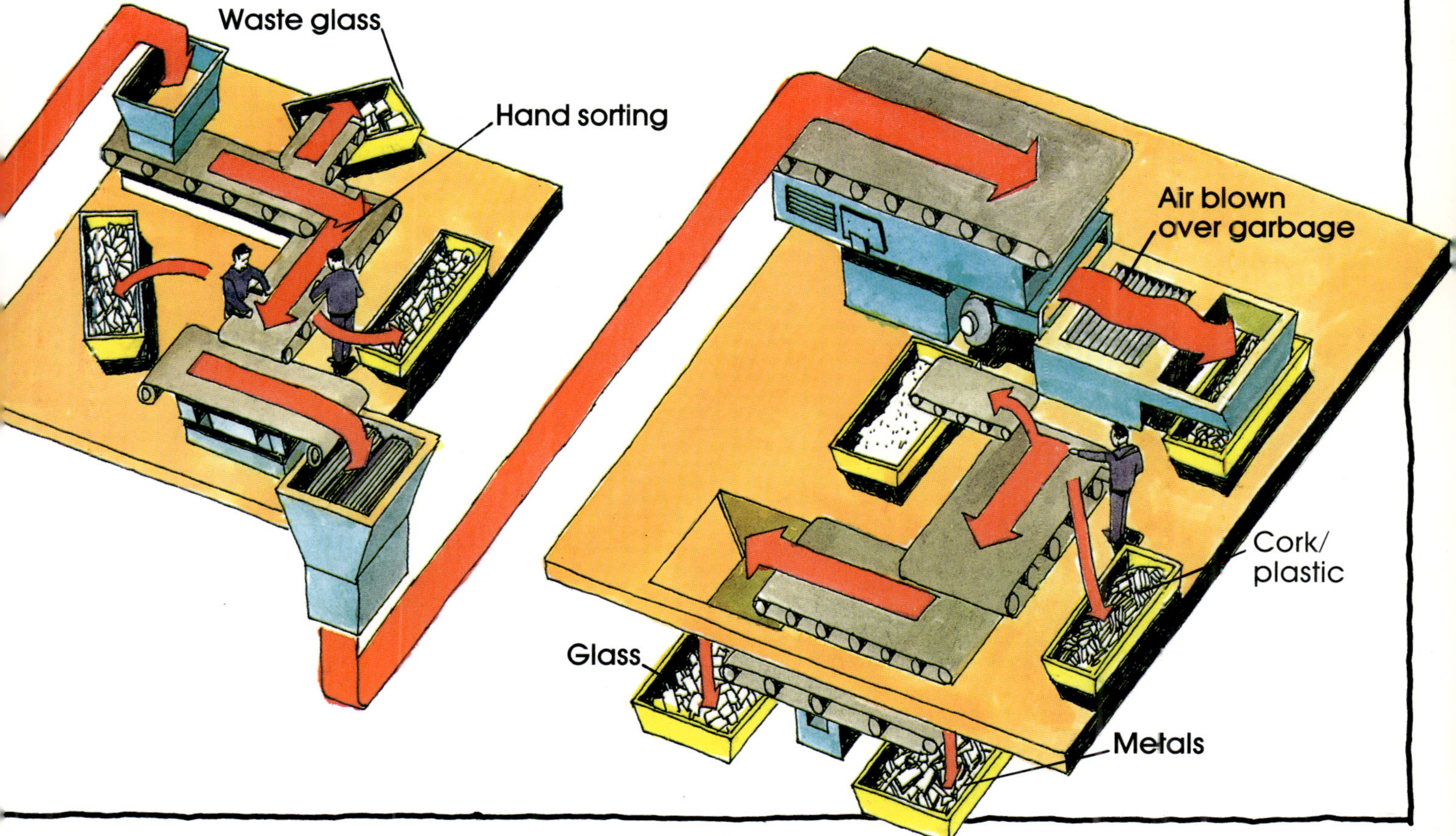

Waste glass
Hand sorting
Air blown over garbage
Cork/plastic
Glass
Metals

Industry

Industry produces the largest amount of waste. Many companies are now looking for ways to recycle their industrial wastes, or reuse them to make new products. In Sweden, the government helps companies to find buyers who can use their dangerous wastes. Scrap metal can be melted down and made into new products. The German car firm BMW has developed a car made almost entirely from recyclable materials.

Recycling industrial waste does not just save resources and energy – it can also save industry money, which may encourage more businesses to become involved in it.

Useful industrial substances like solvents – which dissolve materials in the same way as water dissolves salt – can be collected after use, cleaned up and used again.

Toxic wastes are produced during the making of video tapes. This waste is sold to fertilizer makers, who convert it to plant food.

Energy from waste

Some types of waste can be used to produce energy. One of the most controversial examples of this is in the nuclear industry. Fuel rods containing uranium provide energy for nuclear power plants. When the rods reach the end of their useful lives, they still contain large amounts of uranium. The uranium can be taken out and used to make new fuel rods.

This power plant (left) is burning old tires from cars and trucks to produce power.

Power from tires
Every year millions of worn out tires are thrown away. However, they can be safely burned to produce power. The rubber from tires can also be recycled to make things like pipes and doormats.

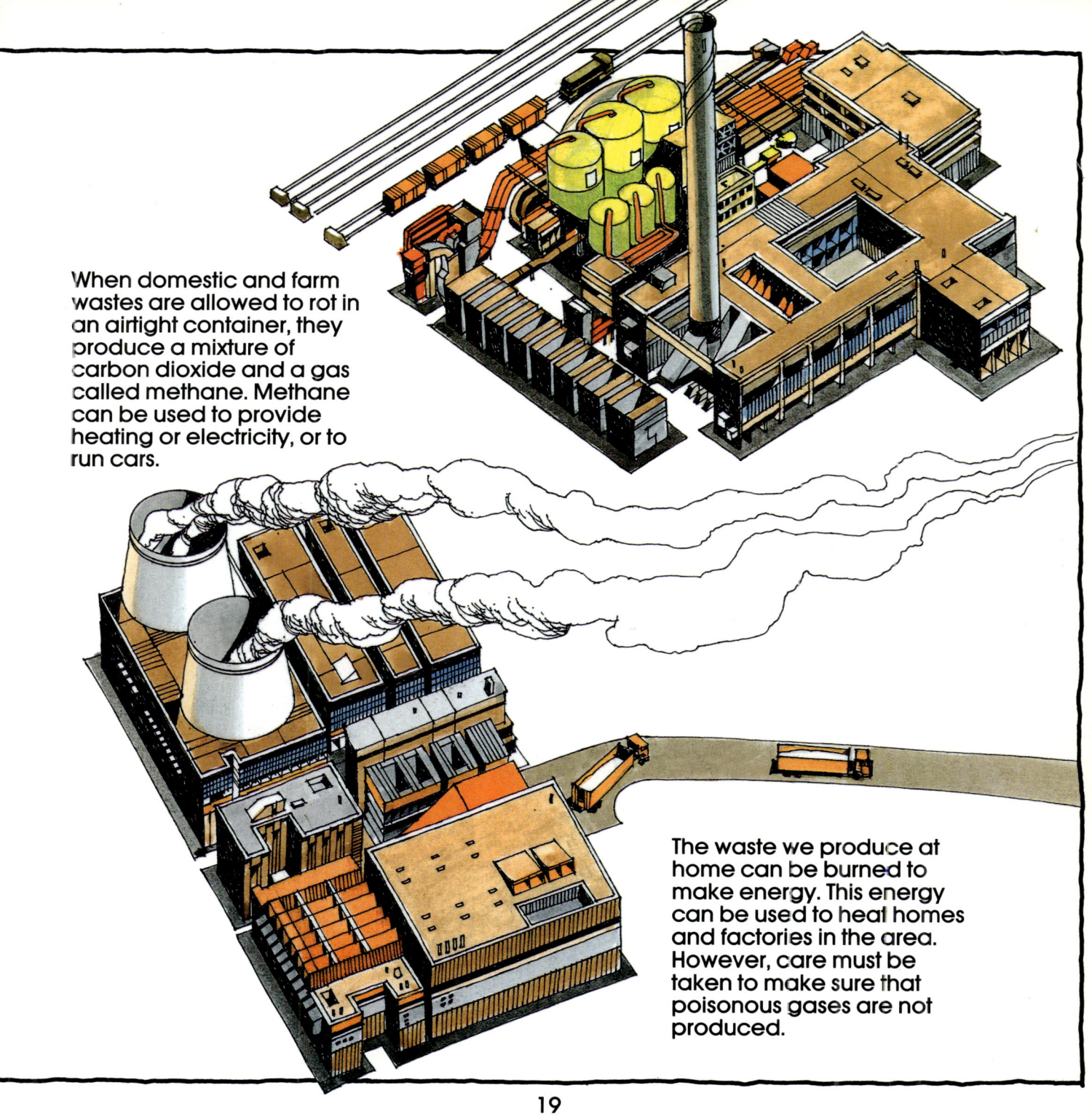

When domestic and farm wastes are allowed to rot in an airtight container, they produce a mixture of carbon dioxide and a gas called methane. Methane can be used to provide heating or electricity, or to run cars.

The waste we produce at home can be burned to make energy. This energy can be used to heat homes and factories in the area. However, care must be taken to make sure that poisonous gases are not produced.

Plastics

Plastics are extremely useful materials. But they do not easily break down, and it is difficult to separate the different types for recycling. In the United States, the polystyrene from fast-food containers is collected and recycled. However, projects like these are rare, and most plastic is burned or buried with other garbage.

Some types of plastic melt when heated and can be reshaped into new products. For example, beverage bottles can be recycled into road cones and fence posts.

Many different things are made of plastic: bottles, packets, toys, and ballpoint pens.

In Germany, some bottles are made from a type of plastic which breaks down in strong sunlight or when buried. But the bottles are expensive and they may break down while they're being used.

Recycling worldwide

Recycling takes very different forms throughout the world. In wealthy countries like the United States and Britain, where most waste is produced, recycling is being encouraged as a way of reducing waste and preventing pollution. In poorer countries, however, most people cannot afford new materials, so everything of value is reused many times. Items that have been thrown away, like tires or even light bulbs, are turned into new products, so very little waste is made.

In some cities around the world people live on or near dumps, and collect waste from them to use for themselves or to sell.

In some wealthy countries special projects are being introduced to encourage recycling. In most areas, there are collection points for materials like cans, glass, and paper, and these may even be collected door to door. Some small towns and villages may even have mobile recycling centers.

Plenty of available collection points encourage people to use them rather than throwing things away.

What can you do?

One of the simplest and most effective ways to deal with waste is to produce less of it. However, once the waste exists, there are many ways of recycling it. Some councils now organize collection points for materials that can be recycled, like newspapers, cans, and glass. Paper bags and plastic bags can be reused, and charities use old stamps and aluminum foil for fundraising.

Bottles and glass

General garbage

When food scraps and garden waste are put onto a compost heap and covered, they rot down to make compost.

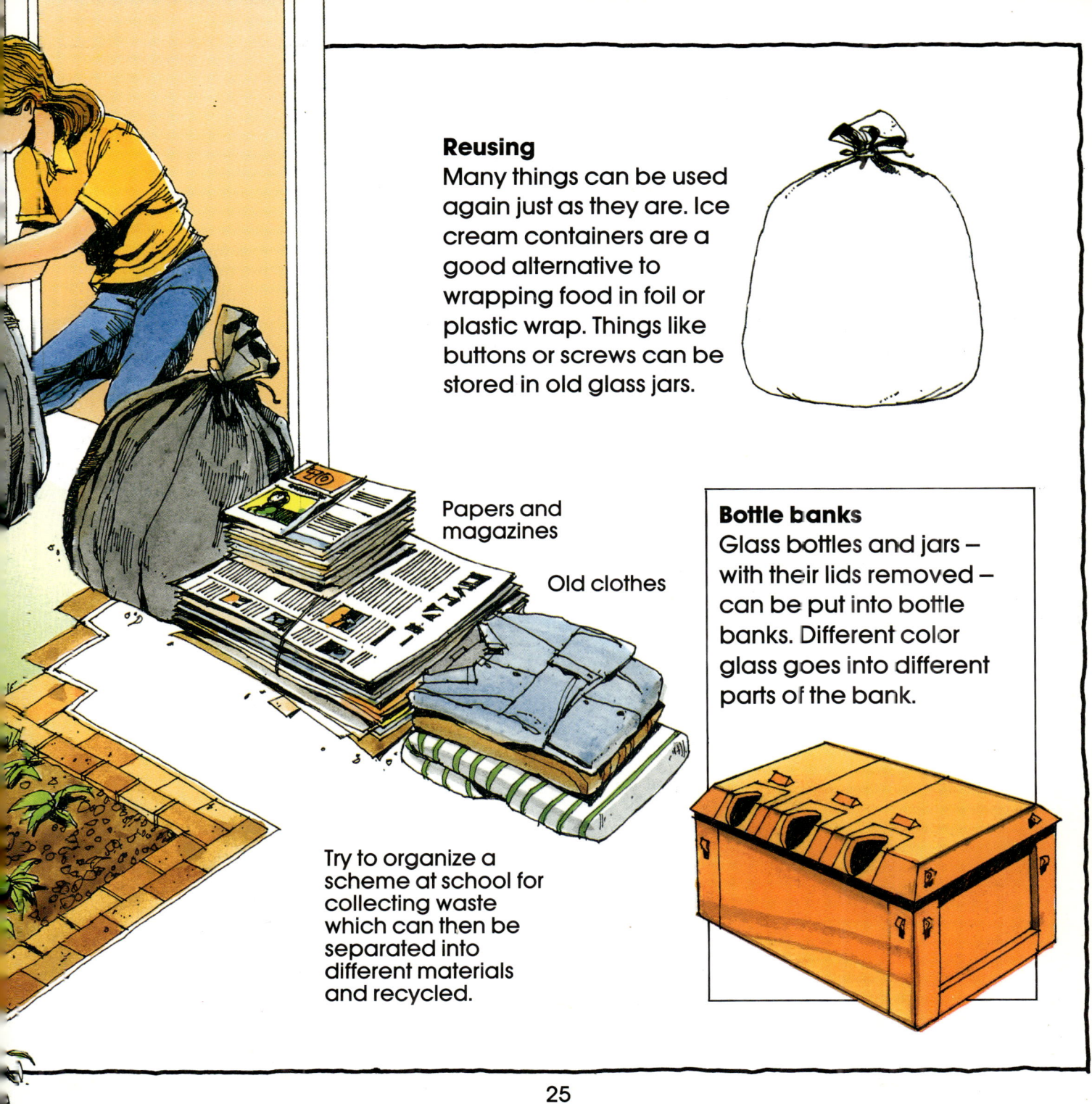

Reusing
Many things can be used again just as they are. Ice cream containers are a good alternative to wrapping food in foil or plastic wrap. Things like buttons or screws can be stored in old glass jars.

Papers and magazines

Old clothes

Try to organize a scheme at school for collecting waste which can then be separated into different materials and recycled.

Bottle banks
Glass bottles and jars – with their lids removed – can be put into bottle banks. Different color glass goes into different parts of the bank.

Making it work

To make recycling work, everyone has to make an effort. People can persuade manufacturers to produce less waste by buying goods that can be recycled or reused, and by avoiding things with too much packaging. Governments can do more to encourage industries to recycle and reduce their waste. Recycling may cost a little extra time and money, but it is an important way of reducing the damage caused by mounting piles of garbage.

Factories can be forced to pay for the waste they produce. This money can then be used to develop new ways of recycling.

Efficient separation and collection programs, both at home and in industry, would make recycling quicker and easier.

Sewage sludge can be used as a fertilizer on the land if it is not mixed with the poisonous wastes from industry.

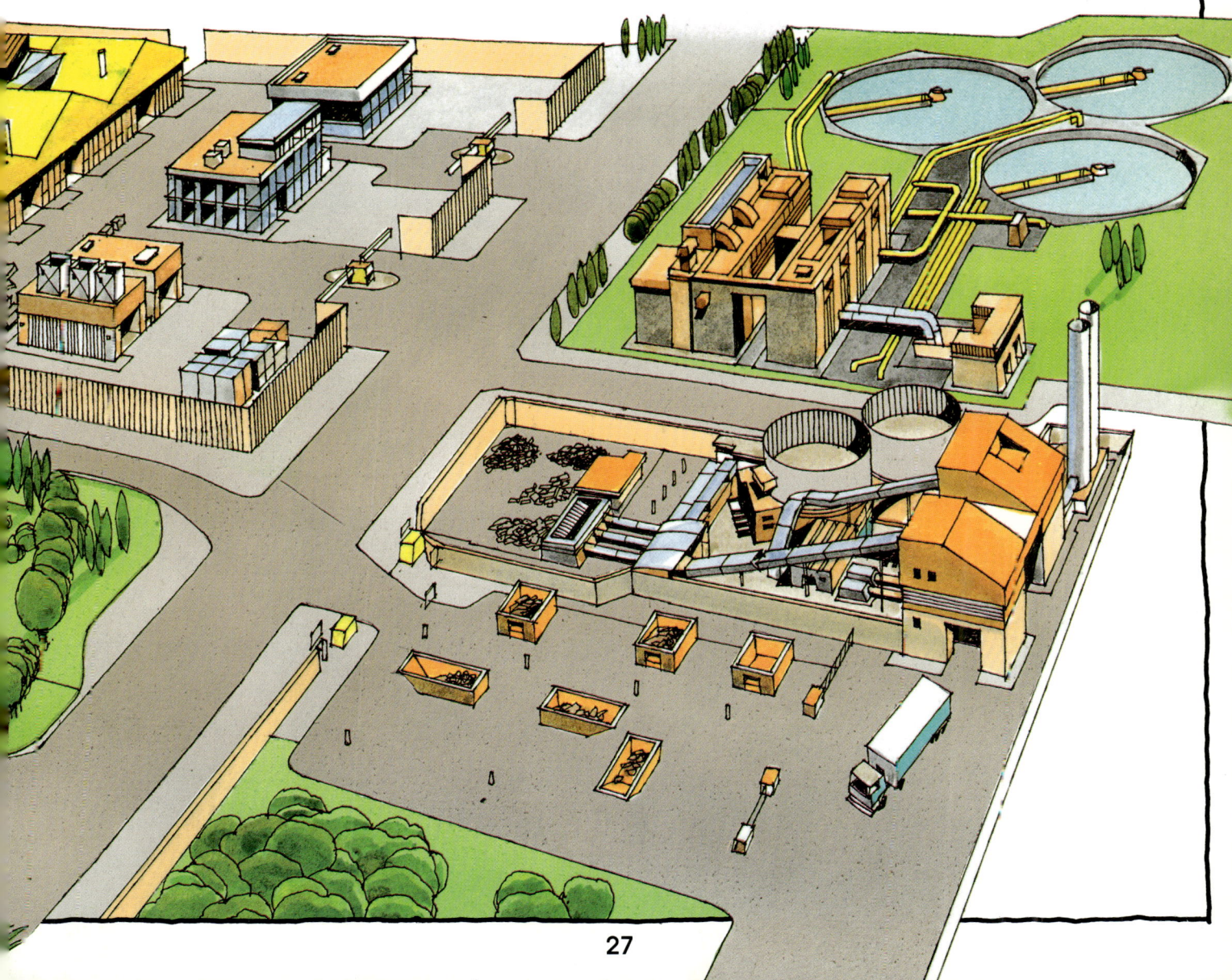

Did you know?

Some wastes can be recycled by tiny waste-eating bacteria. Poisonous waste from oil refineries can be plowed into the soil, where it is broken down into harmless substances by bacteria. In Germany, millions of old Trabant cars lie on rubbish dumps. Trabants are made from a wood pulp mixture that could be broken down by bacteria.

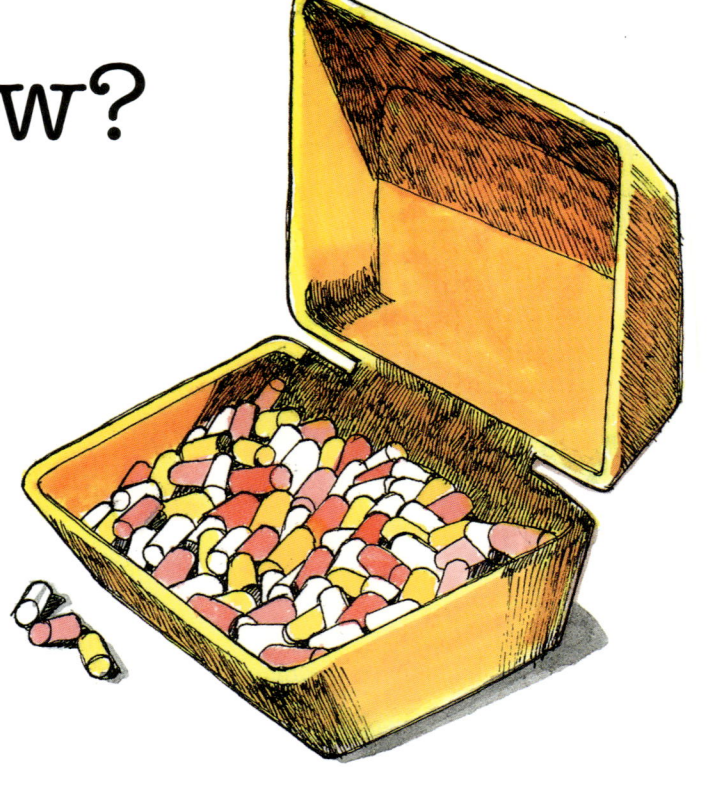

The plastic containers from fast-food restaurants contain harmful gases called CFCs (chlorofluorocarbons) which damage the ozone layer. Many of these containers are now being collected and turned into tiny pellets. The pellets can be melted to make new products, or used in the building industry.

Every family in the United States throws away about eight trees' worth of paper every year. Yet paper is one of the easiest materials to recycle. At the recycling plant the paper is made into a porridgy pulp with water, then dried and rolled out to make new paper and cardboard.

Glass is made from sand, limestone, and soda ash. All of these materials are fairly cheap and supplies are plentiful. However, they still have to be dug out of the ground, and mining them can damage the environment. Recycling glass saves 25 percent of the energy needed to make new glass.

Huge areas of wild, open land are often developed to plant the trees needed to make paper. The land may have been home for thousands of different plants and animals. Yet when it is cleared, it is often replaced with just one type of tree. Only the animals that can survive in such conditions can stay there. Many others lose their home.

Telephones are made from many different materials, like plastic and metal wires. In many cases, it is considered cheaper to make items like telephones from new materials, instead of collecting and reusing the old ones. One solution is to label the different materials so that they can be easily identified when the object is taken apart.

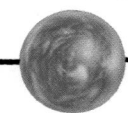

Glossary

Energy
Energy is what we use when we do anything. People use energy to walk and run and even to think. Houses and factories use a special type of energy called electricity.

Industry
When people make many of one particular thing, especially when they make it in a factory. Many products are made by industry, including cars, refrigerators, paper, glass, and plastics.

Recycling
Using things again rather than throwing them away. Paper, glass, kitchen waste, and materials used in factories are among the many things that can be recycled. Usually things have to go to a special place to be recycled — kitchen waste goes to a compost heap, for example, and glass to a recycling plant.

Resources
Anything that is useful. Natural resources include oil and coal. However, supplies are limited and may run out.

Reusing
A type of recycling where things can be used again just as they are. Clothes can be reused by being passed on when people are too big for them. Jars can be reused when they are empty. Even yogurt containers can be reused — they can be used to hold pens and pencils.

Index

B
bottles 9, 10, 12, 13, 20, 21, 25

C
cars 4, 10, 16
coal 4, 5
collection points 23, 24, 27

E
energy 4, 18, 19, 31

F
fossil fuels 4, 5

G
gas 4, 5
glass 13, 14, 29

I
industrial waste 16, 17, 26, 31

M
materials 10, 30

metal 4, 5, 10, 12-16

N
natural recycling 6, 7
nonrenewable resources 4, 5
nuclear energy 18

O
oil 4, 5, 28

P
packaging 8, 11, 20, 28
paper 11, 13, 14, 29, 30
plastic 4, 10, 20-21, 28, 30
pollution 3, 4, 22
products 3, 8, 11, 13, 20

R
resources 4, 5, 10, 31

S
separating waste 14, 20, 27
sewage 27

Edison Twp. Pub. Library
340 Plainfield Ave.
Edison, N.J. 08817